C0-AUI-930

Overheard
at the
Bookstore

It seems like there's a million more books than I realized.

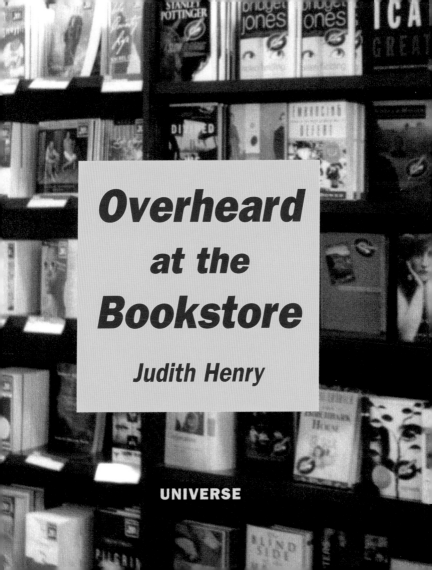

Overheard at the Bookstore

Judith Henry

UNIVERSE

In memory of
Edith Pavese

First published in the United States of America in 2000
by UNIVERSE PUBLISHING
A Division of Rizzoli International Publications, Inc.
300 Park Avenue South
New York, NY 10010

© 2000 Judith Henry

The text is this book does not necessarily express the sentiments of the pictured subjects.

All rights reserved. No part of this publication may be reproduced, stored in a retrieval system, or transmitted in any form or by any means, electronic, mechanical, photocopying, recording, or otherwise, without prior consent of the publishers.

2000 2001 2002 2003 2004 2005 / 10 9 8 7 6 5 4 3 2 1

Design and photography by Judith Henry

Printed in Singapore

Library of Congress 00 134306

Introduction

I love books. Reading is only partly why. Books are good to hold, to smell, to flip through, and to judge by their covers. Browsing in bookstores has always been one of the things I most like to do.

Everyone has ready preferences and interests. You can characterize people by what they read and what they say about what they read. Book selections are personality statements. Everyone has an opinion, and everyone is a critic.

Lately, I spend more time watching and listening to the people than I do with the books. *Overheard at the Bookstore* is a reflection not only of book lovers, but of my time spent with them.

J.H.

You'll never finish that here—why don't you just buy it?

I think I could probably write this book.

SHAKESPEARE

It's not for reading—it's only to impress.

Bring on the next Harry Potter, and make it snappy!

I read all the
Oprah books.

Do you have anything for dummies?

I am not getting you a hardcover book!

I probably wouldn't buy another book on linear algebra and delinear calculus.

It's for my granddaughter, and she's very, very bright!

I like to read the
last line first.

And the
printing
is very
small, too!

Just skip the parts
that are difficult.

This book is so expensive—I guess they charge by the pound.

Should I buy a
Jane Austen or a
Stephen King?

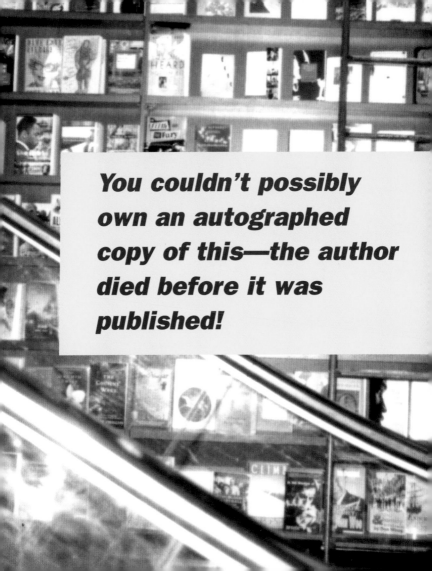

You couldn't possibly own an autographed copy of this—the author died before it was published!

I don't know the title or author, but the book's purple.

Don't think that just because he's in a bookstore, he can read.

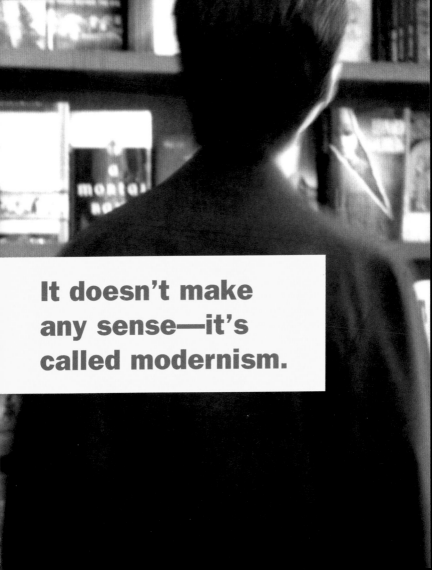

It doesn't make any sense—it's called modernism.

I must admit, I
don't understand
this book at all!

I read only mysteries
and histories.

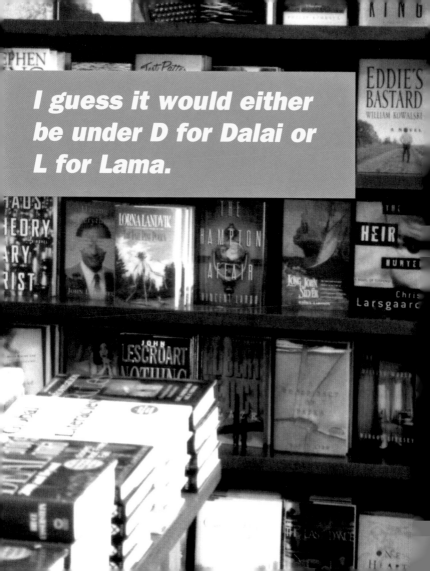

I guess it would either be under D for Dalai or L for Lama.

This was such a good movie!

You definitely don't have it, or you just can't find it?

What do you think Hemingway would say here?

My book club picked this way before the movie came out.

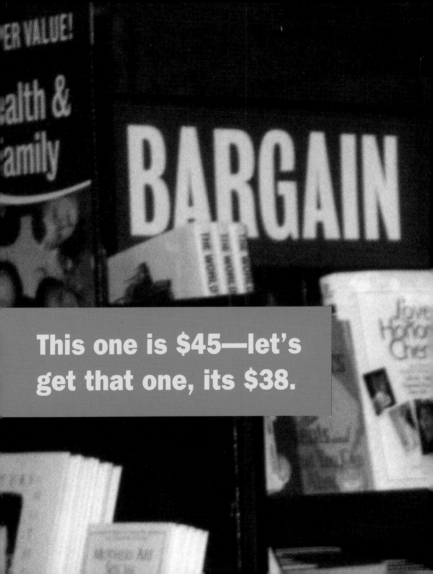

SERIOUSL

Don't buy it—borrow it!

Jack Kerouac

ly people for me are the mad ones, the ones who are mad to live,
talk, mad to be saved, desirous of everything at the same time, the
never yawn or say a commonplace thing, but burn, burn, burn like
n yellow roman candles exploding like spiders across the stars..."
On The Road, 1957

I'm afraid I have to disagree with the reviewers.

I can't stand people reading over my shoulder.

She probably *has* all the Danielle Steels!

The thing I don't understand is, who writes these books?

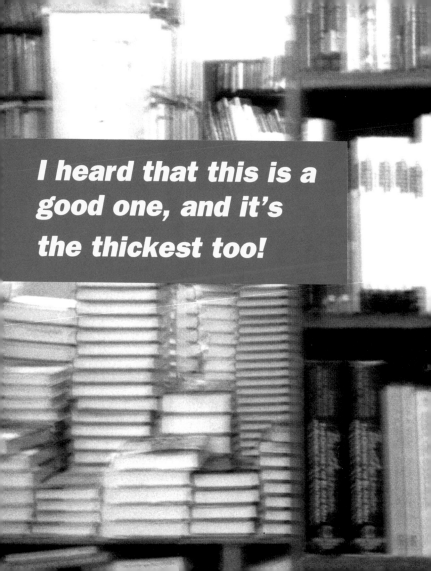

I heard that this is a good one, and it's the thickest too!

It is so dense, but I'm plowing through it.

If it's a bestseller, I probably have read it.

How to Communicate Better, so will you read it?

I am looking for *Conversations with God 1,* *Conversations with God 2,* and *Conversations with God 3.*

I asked for a book on the Beatles and he sent me to the nature section.

If it's about drinking and sex, why do you need to read it?

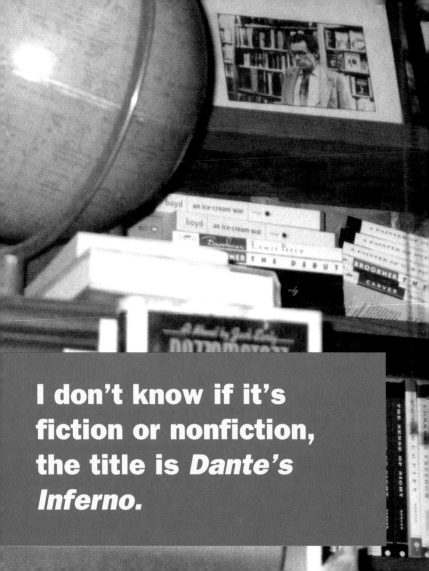

I don't know if it's fiction or nonfiction, the title is *Dante's Inferno.*

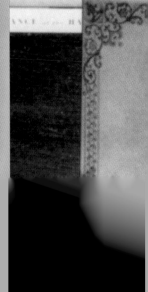

Yes, it's over 700 pages and yes, I read it in one night!

It seems as though everyone is reading *Swann's Way.*

Come on, let's go—you shouldn't read standing anyway.

**For someone
who's supposed to
be a wordsmith,
it's pretty awful.**

This last story rips
me to shreds.

A little reading material for the weekend, huh?

I mean a kid might like Huck and Jim but they wouldn't really get it.

Tommy thinks he *is* Holden Caulfield.

INTERNATIONAL COOKING

INTERNATIONAL COOKING

If I tell you that this book changed my life, will you read it?

Beauty Matters

LIFE THE MOVIE

NEAL GABLER

I can't conceive of how *Moby Dick* became a classic—it's so boring!

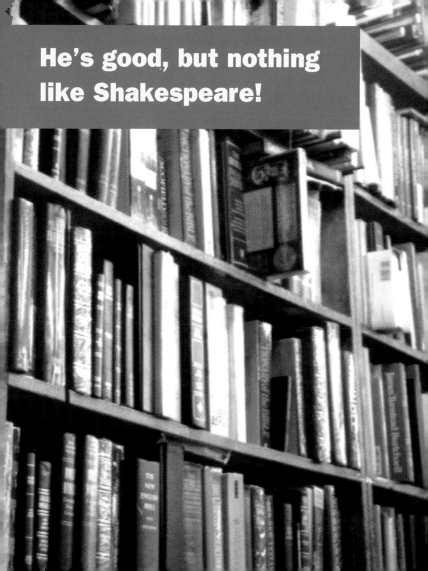

He's good, but nothing like Shakespeare!

This has 39 poems
in it and only one
that is not totally
brilliant.

J. K. Rowling just
keeps getting better.

So all your money
goes for books, but
food's important, too!

So find something
he *hasn't* read.

But Dad, I never read children's books!

Did he write any
big, big books?

Marsha can't get past the first paragraph in any Faulkner book.

Five hundred and
sixty pages and not
a superfluous word!

We had 300 copies but we sold one.

That's a really bad beginning!

They're not here for you to read—they're here for you to buy.

Do you have Cliffs Notes on *Middlemarch* and *Madame Bovary*?

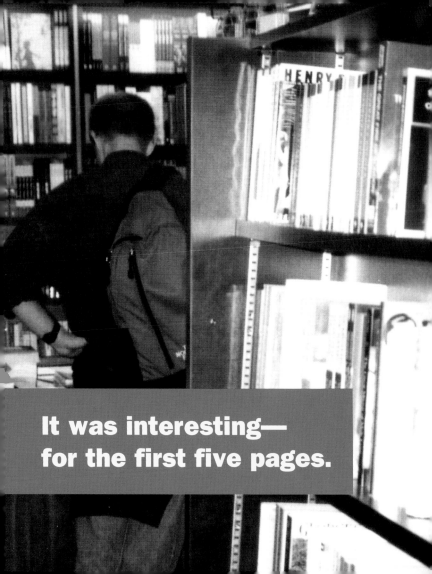

It was interesting—
for the first five pages.

I need a book that doesn't put me to sleep.

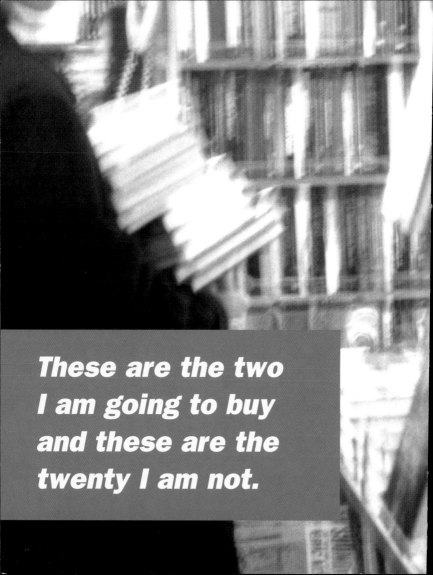

*These are the two
I am going to buy
and these are the
twenty I am not.*

You know where
they have some
good books? Down
at the pharmacy!

About the Author

Judith Henry's art has been exhibited internationally in New York, Barcelona, Buenos Aires, and London, among other places. She also designed works for The Museum of Modern Art, New York. In 1997 her book *Anonymous True Stories* was published. She lives in New York City.